I0835929

Trying to Find You

Laura Klinkon

Designed by Peter Klinkon & Aya Pogrebinsky

Published by kernel-image in Rochester, NY
info@kernel-image.net

ISBN: 978-0-9898201-1-0
First Edition

To my mother who suffered with faith and devotion
until she could no longer ask why

Contents

Introduction

During the time *Trying to Find You* was written my life was an extended period of anxiety, loneliness, and boredom, alleviated frequently by writing. The title poem along with others attests to an underlying truth: my relative inability to come to terms with the existential situation I was in, in caring for my mother —who, herself, had suffered for years far more heroically than I, while looking after my accident-disabled sister. She had struggled and asked why in her later years, tragedy had settled upon her. She dealt with this struggle through doing—to the point of utter self-sacrifice—which, followed by Alzheimer's disease, became her undoing.

I am not inclined to look on high for explanations but have always focused on understanding and dealing with the present as far as my limited experience and imagination might allow. During the time of this volume, I was acting on a few basic principles that today may be thought of as romantic or impracticable: I believe that parents should be honored and taken care of, that children should not simply be left to their own "growing pains," and that families should try to stay together.

In *Trying to Find You*, I am not proselytizing, but reporting, on how it felt to follow these principles over its approximately seven-year span. For myself I sense these poems will in future help me deepen my understanding of this period in my life. I hope that readers who have experienced similar times, may at least find companionship in these poems, while those who have not had such experiences may gain some insight into what they may mean existentially. Perhaps the most palpable message of this volume is that through the creative arts one may get a start in confronting life's questions, sufferings, and losses—even if not ultimately resolving them.

Laura Klinkon, August 2013

The rain pours as it never has

The rain pours as it never has——no matter
that I fitted out the gutter——it pours
lavishly, splashing all over, possibly
unsettling the fundaments of this place.

My sons together riding in this rain,
under myriad glaring lights and flashes—
yes I do ask myself—what do they see
before them in this hungry copious night?

Now the rain leaves broken trickles,
thunder utters distant guttural sounds.
'Round her house the specter of a woman
still scatters life with ashen resignation,
lady's slippers withering at the fence. She
hovers, swathed in pale surrender, searching
awaiting her turn to ascend. My sons
reviled her.

Yet, driving——hungry for they know not what
(not stopping for direction), alert for
ascension, owl-eyed in darkness, they search—
each drop a gleaming window, veiled screech a
convocation, the downpour a flood-stream
of destiny.

It is dark, and though I arranged the gutter
to guide the flow away, it gushes
supra-gutturally, undeflected,
jostling these fundaments.

There was a time

There was a time
when my jade's roundness
did not confound
itself with the ivy's
nor adopt the purple
of the Swedish underleaf.
There was a time when
I didn't know
I could by cutting
the aloe
obtain a balm for
soothing.
It hadn't occurred
to me
once
that
having drawn
the curtain
I would uncover lurking
ominous
effusions.

Doves and penguins

When I was young we'd often wear shirts
with flaps out at the sides—I had
one with a cute round collar
imprinted with penguins.

The doves in the Song of Solomon then
held a special sign for those of us
who could imagine them
flapping in ecstasy.

Today kids wear wings like
carnival heraldry on fitted t-shirts
or as badges of honor etched on bare skin—
their glorious spans appear to shimmer
though thin arms clip more acutely
than in a march
of penguins.

Still others sport cooing pairs
as entrance stickers or as pledges
of belonging, while in cozy bedrooms, beaks
are nipped, feathers neatly tucked
into crafted wreathes——contrite
shackles daintily frosted
by Antarctic winds.

Sins of the fathers

Sins of the fathers
visit the sons? I don't know.
Surely not so much
as the pall's fall when sons
no longer visit their mothers.

Smirking chimera,
slant eyes, sharp crest, rising haunch,
please you to go now.

Life goes on

The poinsettias
growing in still unchanged
water,
two stems propagating,
seeming to love it,
nearly entwined—
mutually offering strength.

The aloe,
waywardly stretching,
reaching toward the lamplight,
toward the narrow opening
in the improvised drape,
toward the ceiling light
erratically blinking—
see the offshoots on its shady side?

The Swedish ivy,
fanning out
laterally as it usually does, but
in a single direction,
because we haven't turned it;
nonetheless,
it's brandishing new branches:
life goes on.

And today my oldest
having brought groceries
since I haven't the car now,
got extra things

we both would like—
no need to ask!

And my younger son happy in
the fruits of a favor he's done,
offers another
without exchange:
life goes on.

My mom
now accepts
the food she patly
refused earlier—
no fuss.
Life goes on.

Non-fortuity

Limited time.
What's important?
Yogurt at Wegman's?
Eggplant at Aman's?
Something to wear?
I'd wanted to see if
they'd discounted their
star magnolia; and,
that's right, I'm
completely out of ankle-socks.
Doesn't seem a fortuitous day.
Got up late.
Only just re-adjusted the sheets
for Mom.
This party tonight
for an uncle I know isn't
overly fond,
my cousin there
inexplicably contrary....
Going because
I haven't seen these people
for eons, and the
out-of-towners wouldn't
have time to stop by.
A present.
A book that had been
given me I'd
go through hoops replacing?
A hand-typed original story about
him I'd written in college?

Would he appreciate?
My copier's out of ink.
Oh, forgot my knee-highs!
And those guys I'd asked
if we had an extra daylight hour yet,
reared as if I were propositioning them!
No, no phone calls today
for Obama!
It 's not a good day.
Arthur's copier
stuck, too. I'll simply have to
tell Uncle about it. Now
how do I get there? Private
even from Google?
Straight, chilly road.
Wow, my headlights
scan the mail box numbers
really well.
Aouah! Awful indigestion——
deli food
combined with Lister.... Oh my god!
That Jeep in my crosshairs!
What!!?
Damn! and only two mailboxes
to go!
So, you, you don't want to give me
your info?

Family at the throttle

So, the media is my family now.
I wonder how Obama liked his trip,
why Michelle didn't go, how it felt
talking to all those people.... On the
lookout she's wearing the right
clothes, striking the right pose—
better send an e-mail today
not to overdo the big flowers.
Friends from around the world
give me advice on how to raise my sons,
the dope on nursing homes abroad,
insights on marital relationships in Africa.
Locally a lady sends me jokes; my son's
landlord sends penetrating messages from
a deep sea submarine. Meanwhile
I find kindred ties in building with straw,
learning Swahili, stand-up paddling—
what else? Friends who aren't connected?
Just don't have time to be in touch.
Even my kids I pass over in favor of
meetings—online or not—I've got to attend.
Anyway they're engaged elsewhere,
outside our intra-family sound bites.
Somebody said, and I'm beginning to see
why those computer nerds cut off their
genitals preparing to be transported to
outer- or was it cyber? space. Intercourse
is possible on various planes! The ultimate
experience may still be out there! No doubt
they asked: Do we really need our genitals?

I'm going to make cocktail sauce today,
I learned how from Recipe.com
and I could make it every Sunday,
if Yahoo Local directs me to
conveniently priced frozen shrimp,
easy to prepare for any number,
even a party of one. On TV I see
people traveling toward vanishing
destinations, and I weep at the fate
of forgotten tribes—even ready to cut my throat
in protest, though with so many causes—sadly,
I can degorge only once. Besides,
the stories, exhibits, exhumations,
creams, appliances, health admonitions,
all show how human we still are:
luring, surprising, soothing, comforting....
I now fall asleep at the throttle,
with a flick of my thumb.

From the market

Well, I thought I was going to tell you
how whenever I walk into a room full
of strangers nowadays, I retain a dullness,
though not really through any effort,
but a kind of stubbornness, or you might say
a stolidness. I think that's right: to make sure,
I should look it up.
I was going to tell you, but I couldn't decide
if going to the market for fresh air would
be better for me, and now, as you see, I've
given up on that and in the meantime the sun
has clouded over, and well, the stolidness, is
like a cage over my heart, or, a leather bodice, or,
an elastic bladder that shrinks with the thing it's
holding—the bladder being the best analogy, whatever
the true fabric is. So why do I tell it anyway, when
I wouldn't have, having gone? The import, please...?

The import is that rather than go to the market
where most are certainly strangers and where, in fact,
I would be importing myself, while I myself would
be in search of imports: mangoes, papaya, and Chilean
or Columbian fennel, I choose to stay and speak
with someone I know, though I know only myself. So I
speak to the shadow of myself, who I don't actually know
nor seek to discover: What's to discover in a sad, dull, aging?
And can I still? without bringing on peltings of seedy chuckles?

In winter I walk into gatherings wearing my coat. And
I have my teeth to worry about, which seems to be a

popular subject these days: when in the doldrums,
discover your teeth. Indeed, today I discovered
the dental pick with disclosing dye, conveniently purchasable
—no trip to the market necessary—with which, I could
scale mountains of tartar, if I wish. Or whiten with hydrogen
peroxide combined with baking soda—of which I have plenty.
Still, I may resort to Listerine, that, I am guessing,
from the persistent, slightly caustic pulsation,
is spiked with a little of both—I'll have to check.

Well, is this what I have to disclose or uncover? The thrill of
exhuming tartar? It may be the end all, after all. But
better, yes better, is the possibility of telling you about it—
though you be but a shadow. Because, I think it true,
other shadows may follow, and though they enter a room
wearing a bodice or a bodkin, they may also hide
in their satchel a fruit bursting with ripening effusions,
ready to bring home.

Neighborhood sounds

I try not to pay attention to these sounds, especially at night. But I seem to have heard a small screw drop about thirty inches—it came from outside the door or maybe from the crawl space next to the florescent lights. It's two-thirty a.m. Last night a strong wind made a big bang—couldn't see if it was the wheelbarrow hitting against the shed, or something else.

Once it was the next door kid knocking icicles off the eaves, and following through each time with a knock against the house. The same kid who pulls flowers off the hibiscus bushes. He used to be so cute. There was no window on that side of the house. I had to open the door to see if it was a poltergeist. Then, I asked him to wait a minute while I got something for him to bring to his dad, but he disappeared before I got back. Was it a poltergeist after all?

Once a nice friendly kid, with not a bit of mischief. Now he's become observant: While shoveling the walk myself one evening without having called the plow, I heard him snidely comment to his mom: what a lot of work I was doing! His dad is the one who cuts our lawn; he collaborates with the guy across the street, who this year grudgingly agreed to plow upon request. I suppose I'm a threat to their business.

My mother's house where we live has been pelted with mud on one side—all the way up to the second floor. We hosed it once but some spots we couldn't get to remained. Recently, the neighbor boy flew an airplane onto our roof where it got stuck. Without asking anyone, he stood on a chair waving a long piece of hose. He must have remembered our hosing the mud away. But that side of the house is on a slope, and, I noticed, Jimmy could have a great fall. Miraculously he hadn't fallen when I managed to say he'd better call his dad—his mom came out just then. She looked me straight in the eye, scowling with not a word—as if I'd conjured the hose and spirited the toy up there myself.

I think they think I'm strange.

Resistance

That bush,
now why can't I get out there and trim it?
Maybe because it's not mine?
Not my idea?
Not where I'd put it?
Not what I'd put there?
But such is the way of bushes:
they stay and stay,
even though them that
planted them may be agonner.
I'd rather uproot it, that
bush.
Not that it ain't nice,
but that it ain't right.
Too proper.
Look at it there pretendin'
like it's overseein' the yard
while it's only just keepin' that
hill from eroding—not even by itself
but with the railroad ties that hold it up too.
Just lording it over like an
unsheared hobo,
defiant against the creepin' shade of the
unpruned pear.

I'd like to make a meadow of that lawn,
but how to make a proper meadow—
with rivulets
and spring-like fountains?
How to bring or make rocks that will

look like they naturally belong
in this sea of clean shaven
lawn grass?

I actually don't have the strength to move
boulders,
nor even the strength, moral or not,
to gingerly trim.
I prefer to mow things down
and root things up,
to start anew—
to find the strength
I'm sorely lacking.

It's not that my dad chose poorly,
he just didn't choose for me.
And now I'm too old to bring these plantings
to the next level—
'ratchet them up a notch,' as they say.

I would be looking for significance beyond this
uncut bush,
but the only one I see, is that it's there,
and just not mine.
Didn't ask for it to be there,
not reflecting me.
So, lacking strength, I'll let it
grow to its damnation,
and that will be the essence of my husbandry.

And now, I will turn, hoping not to see, lest coming upon

some further significance of this phenomenon,
I will have to deal with it,
or coming to understand that trimming is the ultimate
solution, accept it with resignation,
continuing all the while to resist,
resist, resist.

Notice

The Offenburgerblatt
writes death notices large
even when the subject
is young with many friends,
bright eyes no doubt dimming
maybe wishing they needed
a magnifying glass
instead of a tissue box
to barely grasp in print
this smeary event.

Tocsin

What is this
Rising at the throat
Muzzling at the mouth
Sinking of the breast
Knotting at the gut
Thump, thumping
Of the heart
Knitting at the brow
Widening of the eyes
Hunching of the back
Holding of the
Breath
Running Hollowing
Capsule
Not to be
Detained?
As if
Jaws were to be readied
Speaking deferred
Ribs to give way
Galloping muscles fastened
To contain entrails
Riveted to restrict
Sound
Wonder
Transformed to horror
Paling
For lack of air
Where will it
Go?

Where will it end?
I follow, follow to the rose garden
Where the world's whimper
Chimes, chimes again
Like a tocsin.

Sore throats

I used to be so gratefully impressed by Mom's
straightening the clean fragrant sheets, her
soothing broths on trays, the sun through drawn
curtains, coloring books piled against large roses
on the wall. My sore throats were a daily blessing
until penicillin charmed them away.

My sister might have declared herself lucky
to have Mom next to her daily after her
tracheotomy, if she only could have said.
But often she would smile when undisturbed
by repeated suctioning, cleaning, gagging.
Pillows regularly puffed, propped, replaced;
light, sound and temperature well controlled,
greeting cards, angels, photos, dolls covering
the walls. On nice days we might go outside.
She'd laugh, we looking on dismayed.
And Mom would fuss and pray.

Now Mom swallows safely only special food,
her Alzheimer's holding sway. It's a blessing
we can feed her. She smiles at times in
gratitude. The broth is skimmed of fat. Her bed
not nearly so neat as mine or my sister's,
makeshift curtains filtering light. Walls are
bright though unembellished, echoing
memories rehearsed in jumbled speech.

My throat catches at times, you'd think in twinging
sorrow, but sorrow turns to grief and fear and dullness:

why the walls are bright, why we relish the light,
why we laugh at Lake Wobegon, why writing paper,
dried flowers, and napkins are scattered everywhere,
why there's such relief in a clear spoken word.

Hug

I see you sometimes
reclining, same
as I left you:
your head slung
gravitationally
left, right
back or down;
you nearly gasping
or chest heaving
though no sounds come;
your t-shirt
faintly sighing,
lids look down.
I'm taken by surprise
if guests speak to you.
The best I can on days
like this: a hug I need
to remember to give.
You say, "Thank you"
and smile wanly or ask
"Where's my husband?"

I'm tired today and
sleepy, the clouds
stirring. Your slippers
come off. Your pillow
rests next your head.
I've skipped this morning's
pill conundrum, though
you now look surly.

I hope your feet can breathe.

I thought I heard the rain pour;
yah, terrace is glistening—
like your pillow now.
We'll open the door
and get a clean cover.
Your lids closed,
a fresh breeze
could bring a hug.

White night

Everything is white:
the telephone
the cord
the napkin it is resting on
the White Pages
the black on white
anthology of German
literature
the paper I write on
the cup I
just finished
the corrugated lining
from a biscuit wrapper;
the wall
is off-white, and
the floor.
I had been
following the floor line
a few moments ago
the shades of grey grout
seeming to flow indefinitely
from light to dark to light;
the curtains on the white-framed
window are white
lace against the black, reflecting
glass;
the light bulb, shining on the panels
bright white.
It is a white
snow-covered night

empathic white inside, too:
the whiteness of
no more radio, however refined
no more gibberish
regardless of innocence
no more obstreperousness
from people you love.
It is the white of release
the white of regrouping
the whiteness of breathing
a deepening sigh
through the grayish convolutions
of a weary, wistful heart.

Getting things done

Yeah, good you came anyway.
You encouraged me to up
and get things started.
Yup, did the dishes so you could dry,
did some wash so you could fold,
neatened the bathroom so you could mop—
all just before you arrived.

And since you've been here, I've
hung some wash, loaded more,
made lunch for Mom, fed it to her,
answered an e-mail that came finally,
saying my photos hadn't downloaded,
and my number'd been lost!
Yeah, got a few things done!
Well, what did you do?
I mean, how was your morning, which
you didn't sound too happy about
when you called? Uh-huh, so....

I had hoped you'd do the kitchen floor
and the folding, then a bit of....
But, well, time is up.
I think I ought to pace you better—
have a list of things like I used to before we
thought you no longer needed it. Remember?
You did start with the shower and
found a brush I could keep right there—
super!

Well, you'd better get home now. Folks
after you for white-lying about being
some place you weren't? ...not to look forward to.
Just remind them you're really okay and
willing to pray to become better.
Amazing how the praying part works—
even after you're eighteen. So.
It was a muggy day. Tomorrow will be cooler.
You did say you might NOT have rehearsal, right?
Let me know, okay?

Spazzola

Tonda per attorcigliare
bianchi capelli
rialzati
sopra occhi e ciglia
bruni
forti sorveglianti
da anni fa;
occhi non solo
di mamma
né di papà
ma della terra natale
e gente fa:
di mia cugina mai
incontrata
e dell'altra scartata
della zia che
ancora sa fare
l'occhiolino
dello zio
che sbircia sempre
l'orologio,
del nipote sorridente
pigramente pensoso
dell'occhio
del Ciclope
ancora lucente
e quello di
Cariddi
in faccia ad
Ulisse
e ancora chissa?

Quello
della muta
Sfinge….
Spazzola tonda
bruna anche tu
sbigottita da orbite
altroché blu
altroché lontani
risplendenti
non più
girandosi
cupi
strappandoci
giù.

Brush

Round for winding
white hair
up above
brunette
eyes and brows
steady, watching
since times gone by;
eyes not only
mother's
nor father's
but of a native land
and people ago:
my cousin's
never met
another's
set apart
my aunt who
still knows how to
wickedly wink
my uncle
stealing glances
at his watch
my smiling nephew
lazily musing
the eye of the Cyclops
gleaming still
and that of
Charybdis
face to face with
Ulysses
and whose else?
The eye
of the silent
Sphinx....
Round brush,

you brunette too
dismayed by orbs
so beyond blue
so beyond far
resplendent
no more
blankly
turning
pulling us
down.

Persons who can't

Persons who can't
can inspire
more than those who can
more than infants
more than those who won't.

Persons who can't
through eyes that implore
or that your eyes avoid
or admire and
only wish
call out to
what you can.

Neither the poor
nor the unable
will always
be with you who
may have only
one chance
to show what
humanity can.
They call to you
reflecting you
and are you
in a different
matrix.

Infants give back
with growth

giggles, visions
without resentment
unlike the unable
who may have had
a vibrant life—
greater the pain
and greater for you—
lives chosen or not,
suppressed.

They say it's what
you do with the lot
life gives you. I say
it's what you do
with the love.
Will sheared of love,
too fragile; love must sustain it;
love of life, of persons, of self.

You must drive
their meager strength
as it will drive your own.
And you will see how tiny
sparks light up the darkest dark.
A plunge into the apparent
abyss, a plunge into
the possibility
of infinite love.

Le persone che non possono

Le persone che non possono
possono ispirare
più di quelle che possono
più dei neonati
più di quelle che si rifiutano.

Le persone che non possono
tramite occhi che implorano
o che i tuoi occhi evitano
o che ammirano
o solo sognano
richiamano
quello che puoi.

Né il povero, né l'inabile
sarà sempre
con te, che
avrà forse una
sola possibilità
di mostrare quello
che l'umano può.
Ti chiama
ti rispecchia
è il tuo simile
in una matrice
diversa.

I neonati ripagano
con crescita
sorrisi, visioni

senza risentimenti
non come gl'inabili
che possono aver vissuto
una vita sprizzante
più grande il dolore
e più grande per te
vita scelta o no,
repressa.

Si dice che l'importante
è quello che fai
della tua sorte; io dico
che si tratti di
quello che fai
con l'amore.
La volontà
tosata d'amore
è strafragile; l'amore
sostiene la volontà:
l'amore per
la vita, persone, amor proprio.

Bisogna sospingere
loro la piccola forza
perché sospinga la tua.
Vedrai come piccole scintille
illuminano le tenebre più buie.
Un salto nell'apparente abisso,
un salto nella
possibilità
di amore infinito.

Gods of decorum

I had wanted to replace
those makeshift curtains fashioned
from guest room sheets. Mom
had chosen the tan diamond pattern.
They matched perfectly the rug
I'd picked without thinking of the sheets.
After many fabric swatches, nothing
has replaced those curtains,
as if repeatedly, Mom were saying no.

At home now, her bedroom,
my father 's workshop redone,
not at all reflecting her—I had tried
to complement the window grill,
brought chairs from the guest room, but
really, Mom's curtains, however makeshift,
harmonize the room.

Unable to explain herself verbally,
the gods of decorum are letting her
have her say, acknowledging a life
eminently true to herself, for here
she'll live it out: I notice, too,
the curtains' burgundy florettes
are not unlike her lips and eyes.

The fragrance of bergamot from bee balm
I happened to arrange in vases across
the room, waft a citrus perfume—perhaps
as across the strait where Mom was born—

the gods of affection intuiting that,
though not a child hailing years ahead,
nor a woman in all her finery, Mom
awaits a family welcome when she
makes her trip back home.

Mom, you now have diamond eyes

Mom, you now have diamond eyes,
blackish diamonds with quiet gleams
of understanding.

And your face shapes diamonds
in the area of your mouth:
never once, a place for pasted
smiles or empty chatter,
your lips align perfectly
with the crease of your brow.

Your diamond contours resonate
in the hips from which I oddly
came, not sharing your primordial
naturalness nor your incisive constancy:
you were always there.

Your hands that never looked like
mine are yet mine like the garnet
ring you gave me, but glisten like
veined diamonds now.

Your feet that betray the grace of
one who never strayed, pray together
in the clear, now slightly bandaged light
of who you are.

I adjust your pillow under
them. They make a diamond mark.

Who did this?

Who was it that
brought that
cut monarda
in here?

Should I be angry
for the reminder?

The straight-up stems,
the red, like lipstick,
the frazzled
hair-like fringe?

The deep green
leaflets signaling
"here I am" to
the Mediterranean sky
of her bedroom wall?

Should I be sad
for the reminder?

Who did this?

Mom's going I

Reflective glances
ingratiate the hours

Peripheral visions
evoke old friends

Cherished moments
enter when called

Kisses whisper
your love abiding

Faithful fingers
smooth frayed ends

Bent head
mulls the music

Tomatoes seek
your sweet pleasure

Mom's going II

Past offerings
reverberate in silence

Rain blotches
shade my eyes

Healing wounds
unheal in time

Closed lids
muffle the pain

Crossed arms
cross my heart

Lips loosen
in deep surrender

Resistant limbs
give all away

Mom's going III

Metal assemblages
await your frame

Clogged locks
confound true parting

Waxed branches
slow your progress

Dried petals
want your scent

Old wishes
form comforting illusions

Shawls droop
in dark closets

Your going
marks my horizon

Something sweeping by

Barley string
pings to the floor.
Onion peals
flutter,
pearly coral yellow.
Mellow diffracted
sun.

The ruffles shade my eyes,
fielding sky and
salted breeze.
I wrap myself in sun,
deflecting snow,
bow and glow:
late afternoon
gleaner
off the floor.

Everyone's gone.
The scraps I bask in
slightly sigh.
Eyes swoon in beads
and whole cloth:
something, someone
sweeping by.

There is a face in the marble

There is a face in the marble
threshold. There is a sigh in the
washcloth used. There
is relief in the towel that dried you.
The hairs are silk that were
brushed from you.

Dreams conspire in the shawl
that wrapped you. Your comfort
beckons in the warmth
of the room. Your smile
rekindles the light that lingers.

A shoulder leans
on the stiff chair's contours.
Precious feet dangle
at the swung-back footrest.
Absent hands straighten and fold,
straighten and fold. I hear
a humming near your bed.

Everything that touches
my eyes and senses,
I wish to touch
again.

Good Friday

Good Friday has returned
on dreary Monday. The weather's
switched our feelings. We
kissed the feet and cried on Friday,
and we would by custom think
of Monday as a glad day
as if we felt his suffering more
than his departure.
But how to be glad when
life is depleted by absence?
How to be glad when even
strong winds cannot return
the one you loved?

Early spring's feeble sunshine
sponges the eyes, its winds
clamping the ears so they may not
hear the pounding. Flowers
exude faint perfume—the unfinished
embalming. We smooth our waxen
temples, as though for someone else,
as though for someone else.

Monday has returned the suffering,
too holy till today: take it
as yours, and mine, and ours.
The wind sustaining, we search
the circles of heaven or hell,
hoping to embrace a savior.

Meditation on the wind

It's okay to blow as the
wind, now there
is no "have to", sometimes
strong, sometimes barely there,
loud or merely flapping
in a hollow.
Threatening close,
whispering afar,
at times,
all breaths at once.

Growing old,
one may become part of the wind,
be the wind—turn by turn,
giration by giration.
I shift my arms high,
shift them low,
side to side—swoop
about.

One moment cook,
one moment walk, one
moment write my memoir.
Crusoe brought by wind,
managed wind, became and left
by wind. We only think we travel by sea,
hang hopes on stars,
on waves, much less on wind....

What could we not do, when doing

itself were mere tinkering?
Doings, chimes in the
night wind. Why not ride it?
No ship, anchors, rudders,
no rocks, harbors. Continuous,
persistent movement, rest. Even,
no will, no decision. "Surrender to
the elements," we typically say,
or might one say "to God"?

Ask what is behind the glinting
opaque barrier? Needless.
Wind departs, comes back,
runs, returns. Do we connect,
need to, meant to not meant
to connect, but by accident
gather and drive, gather
'til driving again?

Some acts, beings, things precipitate—
but ride on, with or away. Others
the wind can't carry: land lubbers,
barnacles, rocks, eels. You seaweed,
suffering the currents, soon soon
perhaps letting go
freedom arising.

Trying to find you

What would it be like to come
and try to find you?
I could request
a stocking cap
and waive the
breast enhancers
making me smooth
all the way to my knees
and specify space to kick—
with flippers
should I need them.
And since I wouldn't know
where to go in that
big murky water
I would dive every which
way hard
to the brink of
the heart attack I would
have had, had I waited.
Then armed with the strength of
if-it-doesn't-kill-you-outright,
do the racer's crawl
AFAP
lunge, head down, kick
lunge, head down, kick
so furiously
the tears till I found you
would enhance the
hydrodynamics
and I'd make sure

the wells of my eyes would direct
the flow at an angle,
through that miasma of darkness.
My form, slithery as algae
would foil the sharks
or, worse to worse, I'd
shimmy head-first,
screwing into the shifting sands,
splaying and waving
my anemone toes
'til the real enemy passed,
 or 'til impatient harpies pulled
me up and whooshed me back
to you—to your
forever arms.

Testimonial for laminate flooring

I never believed it when they said
dust consists of shed organic matter,
like skin or nails, but since having
my smooth new floor, I can see
when I sweep the bits onto my
dust bin, how those tiny beads—like
grains of sand upon a shore—
really could be skin.

It gives me a sense of awakening
in the midst of a humdrum day.
I can see my own dust—like looking
at myself in a mirror—dead!
Or at my corpse in an out-of-body
exaltation. Or a rehearsal: the corpse
rolled onto a bier, deposited or scattered
on a beach, in the ground, a mausoleum,
soon enough to be carefully ingested
by golden scarabs, diaphanous blowflies,
spotted burying bugs, bubbly bacteria,
velvety fungi, and maybe even red ants, or
pinkish sand crabs: rich incrustations!
Who's to say decay will not be beautiful?
"From dust thou art"? Pshaw, humbug!
I'm already a vibrant sculpture of dust!

Gathering dust at various places,
yet self-designing, self-chiseling,
self-filing, brushing, smoothing,
a color-drenched hologram on display
and, have you noticed my patina?

So, who's to say, my camphoric
sarcophage-bejeweled remains
will not be beautiful as I am now—
on this new-found wide-eyed day?

This revelation came about, not by pill
or wonder cosmetic, but by Clear Day
Laminate Flooring. Our favorites:
Barus, Cedrium, and Geranium.

Just quarters

Nothing but quarters any more.
My jacket that I may have ruined
with salad dressing, bringing home
the left-overs, has a quarter
in the pocket along with oil
and talcum powder smudges.
After it goes to the cleaner's
it could brighten up, and
I'm sure it won't have that old
quarter in the pocket. Barely fit
when I got it, now it hangs—about
twenty-five percent looser.

The room I'm in has lost
nearly half its lighting—
unfortunately one fourth of it
just above the place I like to sit
when reading. My brother
started to fix those bulbs, but
we do things a little at a time.
I'll just use the magnifying
glass if I can find it. We
did deliver one box of clothes
today. Soon I'll deliver another.
It's possible to savor the act of
giving like slow food.

And speaking of food, we were
going to split a breakfast sand-
wich today, 'til I decided it was

small enough to eat whole. My
brother paid, but somehow I got the
three quarters in change. Then I
learned he was heading south for
Super Bowl Sunday. It was clear I
couldn't tag along, even hopping off
halfway—to see my Atlanta friend.
Met the cheese store gentleman
who reached me the clean fourth of
his oily hand before we left sashaying
to the stand across the way. I was
apprised of market sandwiches—three
of four kinds available on Saturday.

I have four vases in this room, three
with old blooms and one empty. I'd
bought two eggplants, a quarter each,
three tomatoes for same, a peck
of tangerines for three, plus a free
orange. No flowers—and, oh,
a celery for two! I'm checking
my pocket now, and, wouldn't you know,
I have three quarters!

Meditation on structure

I lunge to my right and end up something
like *The Thinker* without support. The
thought of thinking without support
boggles my burden though my brain
maintains.

I think: How much does my skull weigh? and
my jaw? And, while elbow only hovers over
knee, will I fall? Which way? Shall I
grab a left or right jaw cushion?
a smart consideration for *The Thinker,*
who plausibly had only a toothache after all:
a toothache that could have got him
questioning—should I do something
about my ache or bind my eyes
and play my bluff?

As for me, I'll lunge contrary-wise
and backward—my hefty shoulders ersatz
for an exercise mat. Not even a head
bang as I retain my statuesque position.
If only a statue I'd break, no doubt,
more than flesh is heir to—to be noted:
with flesh and muscles I am tougher than a statue.
Except for a few protruding bones,
I could roll about all I want...indeed my bones
protect me. Consider rolling on your face
without your forehead!

How ingenious is my body! I lunge,

support (or not), roll or sit, founder about in
a virtual tea cup, and THINK! by heaven! THINK!
It's not the muscle, nor the bones, but the structure,
the nest, as it were, that keeps my thinking afloat
and this bird—just alighted on my head—
still chirping.

Robinson Crusoe

Today in the quiet,
between cooking and
putting away, rather at
peace with no one there,
I wondered if I were a
Crusoe, smart enough
to recognize his needs,
having had just time
to collect them before
his former thoroughfare
engulfed all else.

At the store I'd bought coconut oil,
oats and flour, powdered milk and
soy for at least two weeks, coffee
for four. My blankets are fine;
tomorrow I'll go for boots. I've
had more time than he. Next trip
I'll collect for a longer stretch.

No one comes looking anymore,
except the cannibals hoping to feast,
whom Robinson decided to forgive.
Idyllic really: goats and grains,
grapes of his making,
complete with coconut
fat, shifting from tending fire
to tidying to writing
his memoir: a good ol' boy,
staying out of the way.

Like me—but with less time than he,
looking over the waves,
reconnoitering a few pictures,
accepting that all I have to do now
is stay alive. And "have to do" does seem
the key. Looking back, it always was.

Beatitudes

I thought of you today as I watched a man with cancer
cherished by friends say his final adieu.
He looked like you in your last days—even a day
when we stood in the aisle before the marmalade jars
and though we hadn't talked a while, I generously
recounted my preferences, offering suggestions!

You smiled, probably suffering from standing too long,
as probably you'd suffered at the aisle that day
when I hurried towards you in my *De La Renta*,
clutching a fragile bouquet—you obliged me then.
At the end, you came to see me a week early, mind made up.

That man, by the way, had a curve of the neck like yours,
and difficulty walking. You suddenly held me before leaving,
my hand from habit clutching your neck, strangely youthful.

Seeming to see what we had been and happy
we were together, a lady shopper neither of us knew
appeared beaming by us. What did she know beyond flowers
and marmalade? What did she mean?
My cart was waiting and your cane.

At last, you repeated something with your eyes,
I sadly not knowing how to respond beyond
platitudes, feeling they should have been beatitudes.
Still at the end, holding and waving seemed enough.
You obliged me again, didn't you?

Dandelions

The dandelions push up
as my allergies bunch up
and explode in lungs and nose.
The mower pushes
me for gas to burn spattering
sprays of green discharge.

My helper, off working in locales
I wish I could afford, pushes customers
to sneeze at add-ons, exploding tips.
My son's teachers push him
to produce more projects for bursts
toward tenure and hopes
expenses will be paid.

Though a bit ditzy after sipping
my dandelion antidote,
I'll push the mower
over new spring
grasses, flinging compost and
heads-off irritant blooms
making way for smarter,
calming flowers.

Spring day party

Sleep restorative ended
could go out without socks
or make up,
market with
not much of a plan,
could be okay with
just an apple for now,
jotting some veggies in case—
wouldn't it be nice
if all could accrue
their own salad
under the cool arbor
doffing technicalities
noticing the purples
and yellows and patches
of pink; singling out
the mourning dove
for her tail—
deducing the weeds,
soon my planting,
sipping swills of this
spring day's moment.

Today in a pear tree

Today in a pear tree after rain
a mourning dove preened,
modestly blending with fruit and leaves.
At which the partridge came to mind, primping
as it does in topiary imaginings or
artful Macy's windows, voices coalesced
in heraldic song. The partridge, like the
unicorn, is etherealized, once
serving as a symbol
for Christ—a gilded Christ.
Yet who of us has ever seen a partridge?
I ask because the partridge is fairly rare
in America. The mourning dove, close
at hand and naturally elegant
in dovely taupe, perches
on our power lines in family rows,
roosts in the shade of evergreens and pears,
carefully renews her gentle luster,
attentively brooding just two at a time.
The partridge, you know,
is not a tree-top bird, nests and scuttles
on farmland or barnyard floors; hardly
aspires to gilding and awkwardly glides!
Ambitious only to preserve, the
mourning dove exudes commemoration
of the calm after storms, the peace after war,
the matriarch soldiers come home to,
the wing-span of relief when eagles ravage
no more, the sweet, dauntless spirit that coos
grace to America, mourning away
its original sins.

Halcyon day

Quiet and balmy inside,
just cool enough out. The
only call my son's—about his
auto repair. Could I find
a garage nearly two states
away? Easy enough..., I'd
found one months ago. He
forgot. – Thanks, Mom,
helpful as usual! You know
they say there's a shop
closer to work....

Oh, Linda called, too.
– How are you holding up for
the holidays? (This the
helper who didn't like my gloves
for doing dishes.)
– Fine. You're looking for work?
– Yes, though staying close by.
Pet funeral services. Our girls
died—we still hang their
ornaments. I know I can help.
– Your experience, of course,
giving comfort is special.

Got to thinking of selling
gold, whether it'd make
sense. Looked into
home-made foundries: lots
of demos. All silent, but for

street sounds in the one where
the smelter liquefied soda cans
in his driveway, extruding
Irish gnomes! But,
where was the mold?
Hmm..., so much for gold!

The ladder's in the car to
reach the overgrown bushes
yesterday. We couldn't—
my muscle-source saying
he ached from lifting
furniture day before.
Next week then.

My sons arrive Thanksgiving,
have to clean the fridge, shop
for turkey. My *Krimi* waits
at *Seite* seventy-five. Wouldn't I
rather *fortsetzen*? Ought
to make butter cookies.
But that video said
even dairy is hazardous!
Sauteed zucchini's okay—
should I start a vegan
diet? on Thanksgiving?

My brother could be back
from Carolina. Quite
protective of his newfound
time. When is a good time,
I wonder. My aunt wants

the scoop on Medicare,
fearing they'll take her nest-egg,
now she's 85. Wants me
to talk to a lawyer.

It seemed a day with little
pressure. Or did it plainly
bounce right by? If I
make the cookies, will I
need more butter? Oh, it says
one cup per sixty..., hmm.

Memories in a bowl of peas

Adding calamari sauce—
pinkish baby tentacles reach out between
half-cooked peas and soggy spinach,
reminding me how awkward it was
dressing him over his long spindly fingers
and languid new-bird pose.

The bits of white,
his brother's freshly formed teeth—and
bright eyes, after finding the white elevator
buttons, proudly leading us out,
looking on.

The peas pureed
that from six months they
practically lived on, my older son
saying yesterday how much he likes
peas.

Onions, not
nearly enough for the
meal in their daddy's cookbook,
not even for the Zwiebelkuchen
I haven't yet made.

And yes, the
spinach we gelatinized for Mom—
'til its vitamins became superfluous.

The white bowl—
last month holding a birthday pudding
for my nephew's child,
complete with orange-zest sunshine—
acquired from my ex.

Zucchini pasta

When you set a wet, cold dish
on a dry, smooth surface
then add steamy pasta and
hot zucchini,
the dish slides a bit—it slides,
it does not levitate.

Medicine and aftermath

I gaze about me in my doggy state
following will o' wisps with nose and eyes;
they fizzle and fall on the page
my notepad with me.
I tease them about
my whiskers gingerly nudging
so as not to imbibe. They might be
curls from a trimming.
Soon a pattern forms
then others.

Black strokes like ink: I surmise
the shape they want to be, note how
they seem to tremble as I breath.
But now they turn a natural grey
begetting a living wrinkled face
the smooth cheeks frightening.
I scurry behind the pad
this side and that.

There's a breeze now and the flecks
bunch in a corner. They say
turning slightly black again:
Pick me up. Yes, with your paw.
Mold me to the mood you're in
or the fluffy pup you used to be.

Too much lasagna

We made
so much lasagna—half left over
in a pot I fear—it seems
much bigger than me, but the old unself-
cleaning oven, I scrub with vinegar
at least three times.

We had a fine time 'til Monday
when unspoken questions lapped
over roll-ups and imperceptible
yelps shrilled from artichoke
hearts though, unattended, the dog
was not there.

We tossed our disagreements
(bellies over-full inviting indigestion)
as if the dogs had been around.
Since you were bolting, there was nothing
but to freeze
provisions meant for you.

Do you think it was the dog on a short leash
who wanted to wolf the remaining meat
while you indignant hurtled away?

Be careful driving, my love,
do not be distracted by wolves
pretending to be hush puppies
floating in soup.

Blue grid

So much depends
upon my being able
to visualize your blue
phone being picked up
by your skinny hand
the first, second, third
time I ring.

So much depends
upon my being able
to hear your lilting
voice across the blue
electrical grid in
recognition that Mom
wants to talk to you
even amid the static.

So much depends
upon your being able
to understand that
when I invite you to
plant tomatoes, spread
the blue tablecloth, talk of
your girlfriend's eyes, I am
oh so blue when our lives
are not connected.

cf. W. C. Williams

Garlic envy

I did not know there was such a thing
as garlic envy. Though my garlic this year
was quite impressive—
and, T.S. Eliot had spoken of garlic
with sapphires in one poem—which
I hadn't really understood—though
I loved and even coveted the image.
Maybe what he meant was that the two
were equally valuable, and if you were
to have found the two together, well,
more power to you!
Or maybe he was calling attention
to the rich mud where they both could
thrive or grovel.

My garlic has pink hues, not blue,
but its size is considerable: tall beautiful
stocks, large bulbous cloves—which,
from a cooking standpoint, isn't really
so great—since, once you cut it, you could
lose half due to the remainder drying up.
Still, a hero of garlics, and a conversation piece.

– What fine garlic you have, my dear!
May I have a clove or two?
– Oh, a friend of yours loves garlic?

(Mind you, I only grew six plants, each with
four large cloves—quite tasty,
but a harvest of twenty-four does not make

a lot to squander—particularly since someone
has already whisked away a few!)

– So, where will my garlic go?
– I really need to impress my friend, you see—
positioned quite high.
– But does she need my cloves?
You know, there are starters for purchase—
half as large, but more of them.
– No, only big will impress.....

(Which is just the way it is with sapphires!
As well as, come to think of it, those fast-growing
dragon's teeth that bloomed into full-sized armies!)

– Oh, I think I know the lady. Should I give her some
myself?

From a gardening standpoint, if I replanted any of my garlic,
I'd have even larger cloves
next year, and giants as time went on....
My neighbor probably knows this.
Apparently envy is common with garlic
and reputable, too, for as custom and legend show,
nothing gains favor in the eyes of the gods
like a super-sized clove of garlic.

Most likely, Eliot knew this, too.

Jewelry to kill

Today, I
intended to find
a belt and look for
some jewelry.
But the politicos
I attend to
kept jabbing at
my psyche
which spewed sharp
arrows
of concentrated ironies
difficult not to admire:
answers to transfix
the minds of steely-
eyed reformers who
gird their thoughts in
glitzy holsters
ornamented with
a silver bullet—
chrome-lacquered
plastic, noxious
when swallowed.
I eschewed the
belt and fashioned
jewelry to kill
out of my
crystal slivers.

As a poet

I wear my ascot cap or newsboy's hat or cabbie's lid,
my flappy jacket and my knickers, if I can find them,
and I don a searching look, declaiming voice,
and pace from side to side, slowly as a crab might.

I am Bostonian, or Italian alla Loren, or St. Louisian
in a street hawker way, but deep down, I'm Gelsomina
in La Strada. Did she play a flute? a sad flute? I only
have my mouth that trumpets baffled and surprised.

I hawk of necessity. I pirouette for that is custom. I
hold forth because my life, our lives, depend upon it.
Mostly, people like me are ignored, except when we
wear our hat, appear to serve a function, evince a gimmick,
or own a sense of rakish humor, muffled chuckle in the crowd.
Though I'm not a rake and, needless to say, not fake, I may be
a vehicle, a pet, a clown in someone else's show.

It's always so. If I wore a dress, would people
pay attention more? If a derby would they clap with gusto?
No. I want to be a cabbie moving back and forth, presenting
and sashaying for a nearly absent set, who will pay
and hearken loosely to my funny declamations—
at the party, tell their friends about the voice they left behind.

About the author

Ms. Laura Klinkon, née DiLiberto in the Province of Enna, Italy, studied literature and language at the University of Pittsburgh, Pittsburgh, Pa., at American University, Washington, D.C., and elsewhere as part of continuing and independent study. She has been employed in writing, translating, and substitute teaching in various cities including New York, Washington, D.C. and her adopted hometown of Rochester, N.Y., where she has raised two children together with her former husband, Heinrich Klinkon, now deceased. She is a member of Just Poets and Rochester Poets as well as Writers & Books in Rochester, N.Y.; she has read her poems in the Eastman School of Music's Women in Music Festival, and appeared in several anthologies, including *Liberty's Vigil* and *Le Mot Juste*.

www.ingramcontent.com/pod-product-compliance
Lightning Source LLC
LaVergne TN
LVHW051016080826
845145LV00009B/2659

* 9 7 8 0 9 8 9 8 2 0 1 1 0 *